SCIENCE KIDS
Seasons
Spring

Aaron Carr

www.av2books.com

LET'S READ
AV²
BY WEIGL™
ADDED VALUE • AUDIO VISUAL

AV² provides enriched content that supplements and complements this book. Weigl's AV² books strive to create inspired learning and engage young minds in a total learning experience.

Your AV² Media Enhanced books come alive with...

Audio
Listen to sections of
the book read aloud.

Key Words
Study vocabulary, and
complete a matching
word activity.

Video
Watch informative
video clips.

Quizzes
Test your knowledge.

Embedded Weblinks
Gain additional information
for research.

Slide Show
View images and
captions, and prepare
a presentation.

Try This!
Complete activities and
hands-on experiments.

... and much, much more!

Go to **www.av2books.com**,
and enter this book's
unique code.

BOOK CODE

E 9 7 5 7 7 2

AV² by Weigl brings you media
enhanced books that support
active learning.

Published by AV² by Weigl
350 5th Avenue, 59th Floor
New York, NY 10118

Website: www.av2books.com   www.weigl.com

Library of Congress Control Number: 2013934646
ISBN 978-1-62127-493-3 (hardcover)
ISBN 978-1-62127-499-5 (softcover)

Printed in the United States of America in North Mankato, Minnesota
1 2 3 4 5 6 7 8 9 0   17 16 15 14 13

032013
WEP300113

Senior Editor: Aaron Carr
Art Director: Terry Paulhus

Weigl acknowledges Getty Images as the primary image supplier for this title.

SCIENCE KIDS
Seasons
Spring

CONTENTS

There are four seasons in a year.
Spring is one of the seasons.

Winter

Spring

Spring comes after winter and before summer.

Fall

Summer

5

Spring is a time of change.
Days become longer
and nights become shorter.

Near the North Pole,
the Sun rises in the spring
and does not go down again
for about six months.

10

Weather begins to change
in the spring.
Cold winter weather
becomes warmer.

Birds that flew south for winter
come back in the spring.

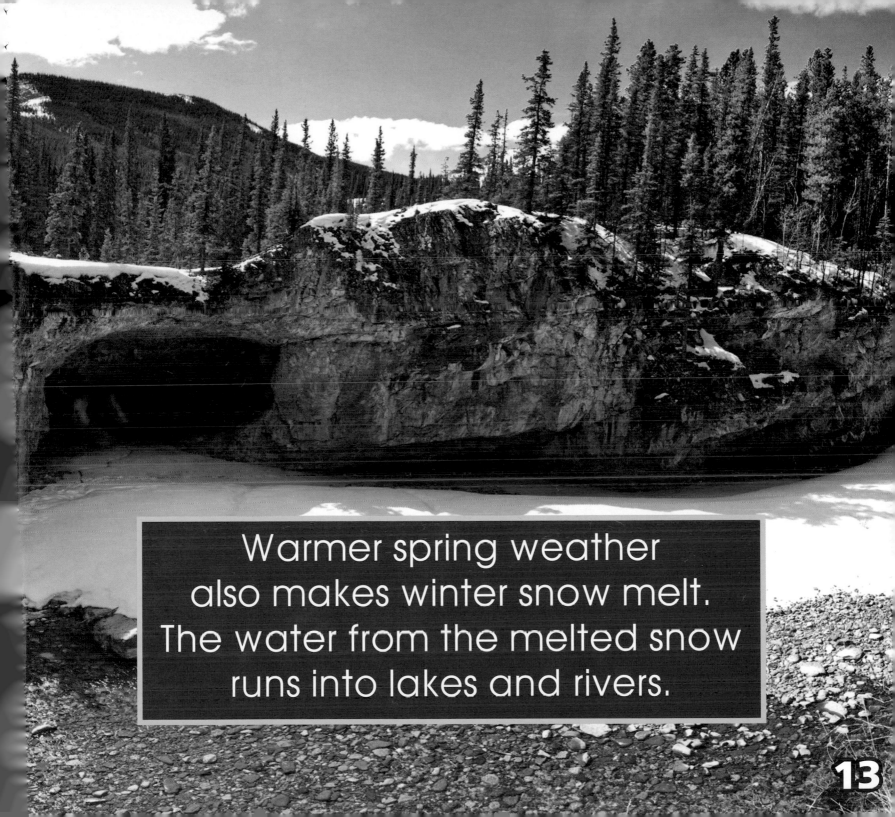

Warmer spring weather also makes winter snow melt. The water from the melted snow runs into lakes and rivers.

There is more rain in the spring than in any other season. There is light rain, heavy rain, and even thunderstorms.

Spring is a time of growth and new life.
Spring rain and melting snow
feed plants and help them grow.
The plants help feed growing animals.

17

Most animals give birth in the spring. Newborn animals grow and learn through spring and summer. This helps them get ready for winter.

Animals that hibernate through winter wake up in the spring.

20

Farmers plant their crops in the spring. This gives the crops plenty of time to grow before winter comes.

Spring Quiz

Test what you have learned about spring. Spring is all about changes. What changes do you see in these pictures?

KEY WORDS

Research has shown that as much as 65 percent of all written material published in English is made up of 300 words. These 300 words cannot be taught using pictures or learned by sounding them out. They must be recognized by sight. This book contains 65 common sight words to help young readers improve their reading fluency and comprehension. This book also teaches young readers several important content words, such as proper nouns. These words are paired with pictures to aid in learning and improve understanding.

Page	Sight Words First Appearance
4	a, are, four, in, is, of, one, the, there, year
5	after, and, before, comes
6	change, days, nights, time
9	about, again, does, down, for, go, near, not
11	back, that, to
13	also, from, into, makes, rivers, runs, water
15	any, even, light, more, other, than
16	animals, grow, help, life, new, plants, them
18	get, give, learn, most, this, through, up
21	their
22	all, do, have, pictures, see, these, what, you

Page	Content Words First Appearance
4	seasons, spring
5	fall, summer, winter
9	months, North Pole, Sun
11	birds, weather
13	lakes, snow
15	rain, thunderstorms
21	crops, farmers
22	quiz